CASPER
The Friendly Service Dog

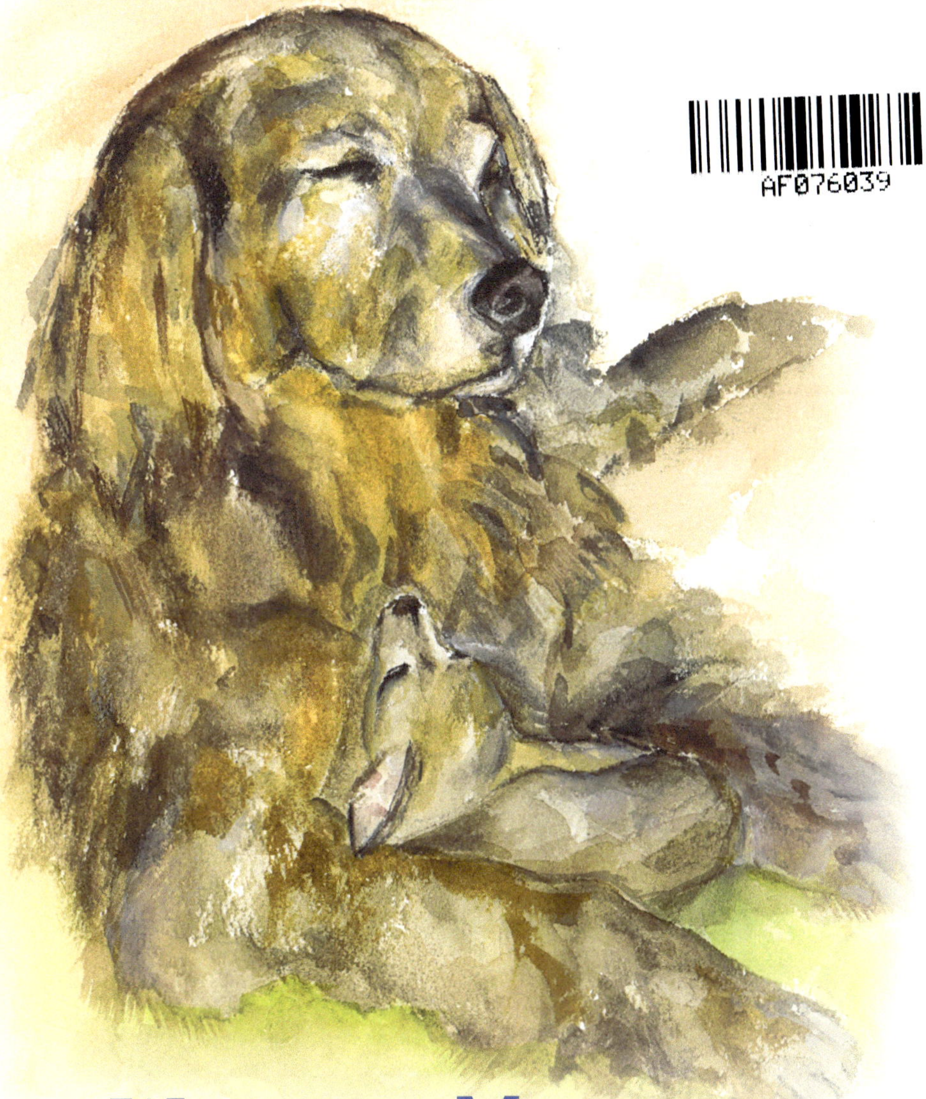

by Wayland Massey

Photos by Ed Massey

Sarasota, Florida

Copyright © Wayland Massey, 2011

All rights reserved. Published by the Peppertree Press, LLC. the Peppertree Press and associated logos are trademarks of the Peppertree Press, LLC.

No part of this publication may be reproduced, stored in a retrieval system, transmitted in any form or by any means, electronic, mechanical, photocopying, recording, or otherwise, without prior written permission of the publisher and author/illustrator. Graphic design by Rebecca Barbier.
Photos by Ed Massey.
Edited by Laraine McCool.
Cover illustration by Madge Fleece.

For information regarding permission,
call 941-922-2662 or contact us at our website:
www.peppertreepublishing.com or write to:
the Peppertree Press, LLC.
Attention: Publisher
1269 First Street, Suite 7
Sarasota, Florida 34236

ISBN: 978-1-936343-73-7

Library of Congress Number: 2011923913

Printed in the U.S.A.

Printed April 2011

DEDICATION

This book is dedicated to Casper's parents, Sharon and Craig Latimer, who lovingly raised Casper for eighteen months before selflessly relinquishing her into the hands of a virtual stranger.

Chapter 1
Getting a Service Human

I'm Casper, a female golden retriever. I have been training to become a service dog since I was only six weeks old. A service dog provides assistance to a person confined to a wheelchair. Having a disability makes simple chores, like cleaning your room, difficult, if you do not have help. Since I was a little puppy, I have been dropped off at K9 School in the mornings. School teaches me how to behave in public places, such as shopping centers and restaurants where regular animals are usually not allowed. I have also been taught many commands, such as how to open and close doors and how to retrieve items from supermarket shelves.

At the end of each school day my foster parents pick me up and drive me home, just as they do for their own children when they finish their day at school. Once I get home, I run around and play with my sister, Harley, who is also a beautiful golden retriever. I chew on rawhide and play like regular dogs do, but I know I'm only allowed to roughhouse when my parents take my working coat off. I also enjoy practicing the commands I learned at school by showing them off to my parents.

At almost the age of two, I know I am ready to be placed with a person who needs me, even though I will have to move away from my parents and Harley. I have been placed with a young man named Adam, who is handicapped. Adam has the use of only one arm, and also has difficulty walking. He sometimes uses a wheelchair, while at other times he walks with a cane. When I met Adam, we played together and became good friends and now I trust him completely. Adam and I worked together every day for two weeks. This made me want to work hard so I could be the best dog for him and he would take me home! Luckily, we bonded, as humans say, and when I graduated from K9 School, I began my new journey with Adam, as partners for life.

At first I really missed my parents, but I knew my job was to take care of Adam now. Adam brushes my hair several times a day, making my hair look pretty and shiny. Adam cleans my ears, trims my toenails, and brushes my teeth once a week with special dog toothpaste, I love licking the toothpaste! I feel lucky to be a service dog, receiving so much loving care without having to remain outside in the heat or cold all day like some dogs do.

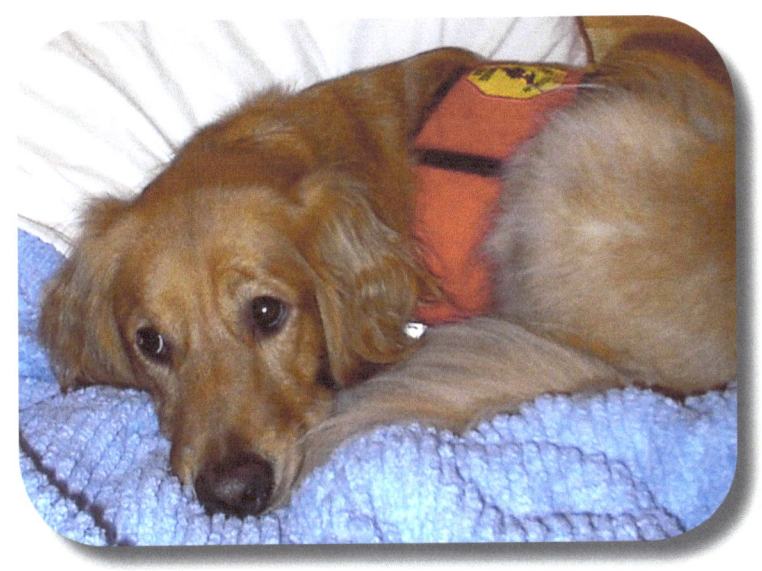

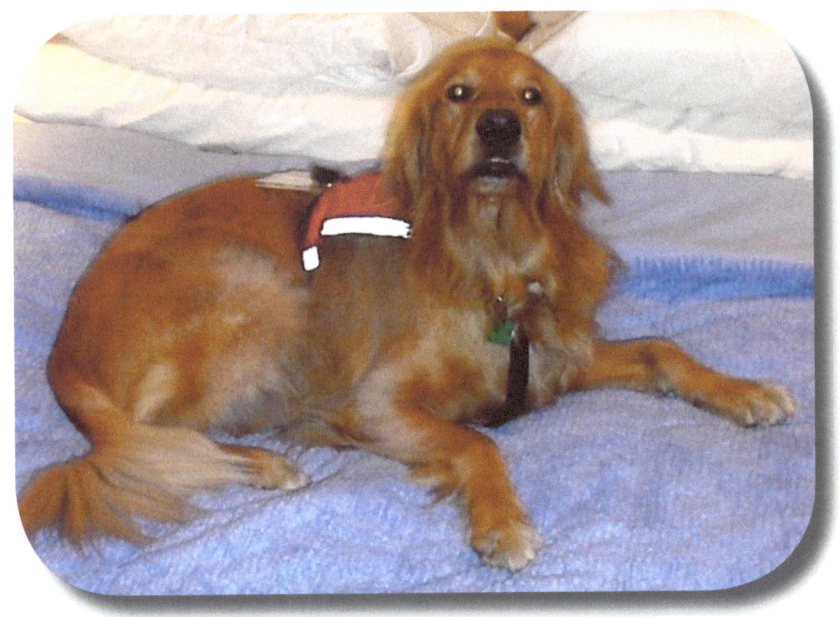

All day long I stay near Adam in case he needs my help; I'm even allowed to sleep on his bed at night.

Adam's family has a Chihuahua living in their home, and I've never seen such a tiny dog before. The tiny puppy is almost the same golden color as me. She follows me whenever I walk to my bowl for a sip of water, or for a bite to eat. Every time I lay down to rest she is quick to nestle against my chest where she feels secure, and is nearly hidden in the long locks of my flowing hair.

Can you spot my little sister in these two pictures?

When Adam takes a shower I relax by the bathroom door until he is finished. When he eats breakfast, I stay right by his feet. After dressing himself, Adam grooms me and puts on my special coat. This coat lets others know that I am a working dog "on duty" and that they should not pet or distract me in any way. People pet me a lot even though my special coat reads "DO NOT PET." If a stranger pets me while I am walking beside Adam, I could become distracted and cause Adam to lose his balance. I wouldn't want Adam to fall down and get hurt because he is my best friend.

Chapter 2
Salty Dog

"Hey Casper, do you want to go on the boat today?" Adam asked. My tail wagged back and forth, like a windshield wiper on a car. I answered, "arrrrr arrrrr arrrrrgh!" I was so happy, I almost jumped up to lick Adam but then I remembered he might fall over from my weight because one of his legs is not as strong as the other. While imagining an enjoyable day on the sea, I noticed that our car slowed down in front of a grocery store. Adam told me that we were stopping to purchase sunblock for the day's activities. Wasting no time, we entered the store and bought a container of lotion to protect our skin from the sun's harmful rays.

Walking on the dock beside Adam is distracting for me because there are so many birds flying by and boat motor sounds all around,  and I know I must remain calm. Boarding the boat is quick and easy for me. Then I turn around and watch Adam, who needs assistance moving from the dock onto the boat. Once we are all safely on the boat, Adam sits down in his seat. I lick him and wag my tail, hoping he will take my coat off and give me permission to play.

Adam smiled and swiftly removed my working coat, while saying, "have fun Casperina!" I ran to the front of the boat smelling the fresh air and watching the birds fly all around as we cruised away from the dock. Adam called my name and pointed to show me where several very large fish were swimming. "It's a pod of dolphins!" Adam shouted with excitement. These shiny gray creatures are very pretty and even bigger than I am.

Slowing down at a shallow area, I looked back to see what was happening. "Casper, do you want to go swimming?" Adam asked. I love swimming, whether in a swimming pool or in the ocean, so I answered with an enthusiastic bark. Adam's father helped him get out of the boat and into the water, and Adam began wading away from the boat in chest-high water. I was also lowered into the water so I could swim and play. Adam asked his father for a life jacket so he could float around easier. His father dropped a jacket into the water in front of me and told me to take it to Adam. I grabbed the life jacket securely in my mouth and swam through the water until I was able to put the bright orange jacket right into Adam's hands.

I swam for several minutes when I heard someone calling my name. I saw Adam

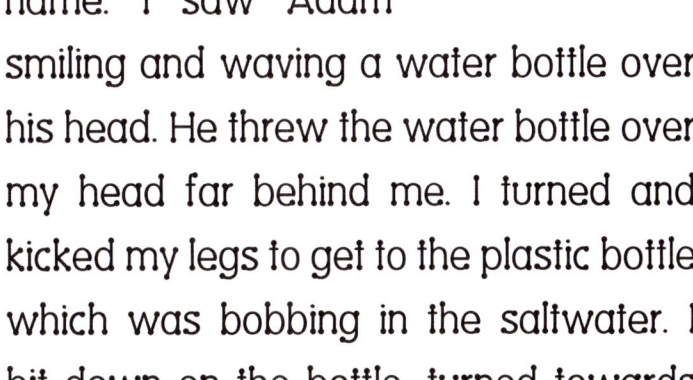

smiling and waving a water bottle over his head. He threw the water bottle over my head far behind me. I turned and kicked my legs to get to the plastic bottle which was bobbing in the saltwater. I bit down on the bottle, turned towards Adam and paddled to him, proudly

showing off my bottle, as if I had retrieved a mallard duck for a hunter. I gave the bottle back to Adam so that he could throw it again and again for me to fetch. After playing for awhile, I swam to Adam so that he could grab my tail for me to pull him through the water. I felt like Flipper the dolphin swimming through the water while Adam held on.

Adam called out to me, saying "Casper, go to the boat." I swam close to the boat where Adam released my tail and then climbed back on board with his father's help.

We saw many disturbances on the surface of the water. "Quick, put bait on the hooks and try to catch a fish!" Adam shouted to his father. Adam casted the bait with a calm urgency, unsure of 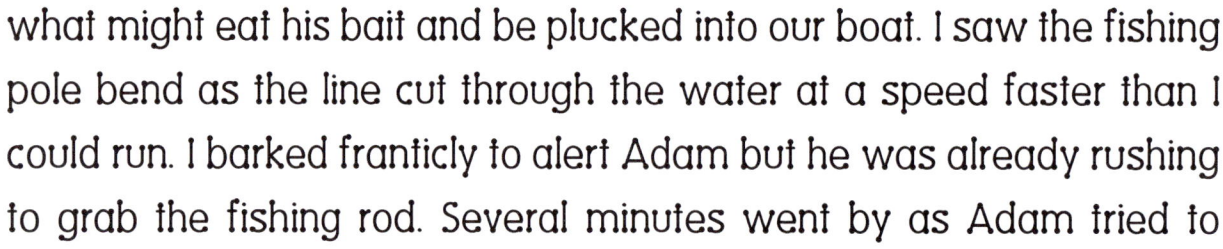 what might eat his bait and be plucked into our boat. I saw the fishing pole bend as the line cut through the water at a speed faster than I could run. I barked franticly to alert Adam but he was already rushing to grab the fishing rod. Several minutes went by as Adam tried to reel in the fish, and finally snatch the long polka-dotted critter into the boat. "Wow Casper, look at those teeth!" Dripping with seawater, the fish's teeth were gleaming white and sharp as razor blades. Adam's father removed the prickly hook, and swiftly returned the fish into the ocean so that he could swim away unharmed. The next hour was solid entertainment as we caught more fish and even some small sharks before we moved on.

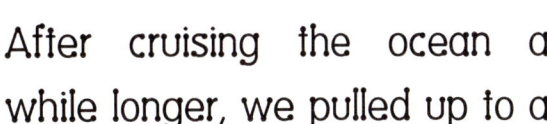
After cruising the ocean a while longer, we pulled up to a sandbar, which had many exposed shallow areas where lots of birds were feeding and resting. At first, I ignored the birds, even though I really wanted to chase them. Then, Adam pointed at the birds and said "it's okay Casper, go and play with them." I had never been happier!

A chance to run nearly a half mile away from the boat chasing hundreds of birds as they were flying away. Soon worn out and thirsty, I trotted towards the boat. Once on board, the first thing I did was to shake all of the water off of me. I must have looked funny because Adam laughed loudly as I was shaking the water from my dripping wet body. As our boat sped back to the marina, Adam said "Casper, I sure am tired." I was exhausted too! I was very happy to have Adam to curl up beside so that I could take a nap before going back on duty.

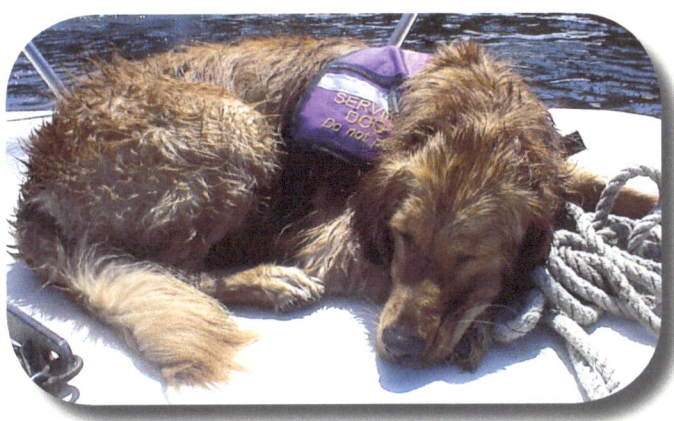

Chapter 3
A Day at the Movies

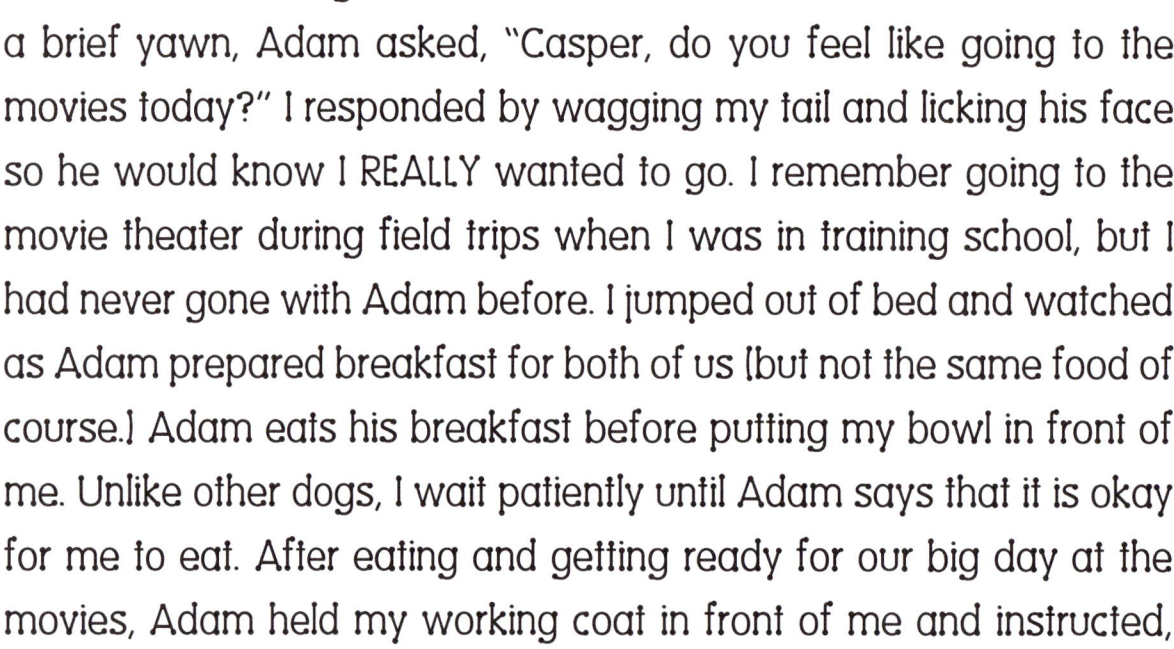

I woke up to see light shining through the window in Adam's room. I sleep close to Adam's legs so that I can wake up when I feel him move. I always want to know if Adam needs to get out of bed. After a brief yawn, Adam asked, "Casper, do you feel like going to the movies today?" I responded by wagging my tail and licking his face so he would know I REALLY wanted to go. I remember going to the movie theater during field trips when I was in training school, but I had never gone with Adam before. I jumped out of bed and watched as Adam prepared breakfast for both of us (but not the same food of course.) Adam eats his breakfast before putting my bowl in front of me. Unlike other dogs, I wait patiently until Adam says that it is okay for me to eat. After eating and getting ready for our big day at the movies, Adam held my working coat in front of me and instructed, "Casper, dress." Wagging my tail in excitement, I quickly walked into my coat, knowing that Adam always dresses me just before we leave the house together.

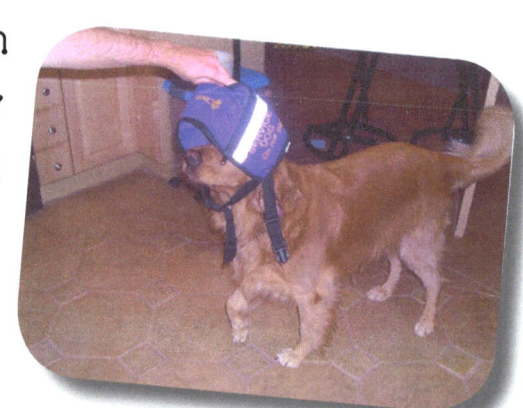

Going outside to get into the car, I know just when to jump in because Adam will open the door giving me the command, "Casper, car!" I always get in the car first and then watch Adam to make sure he enters the car safely.

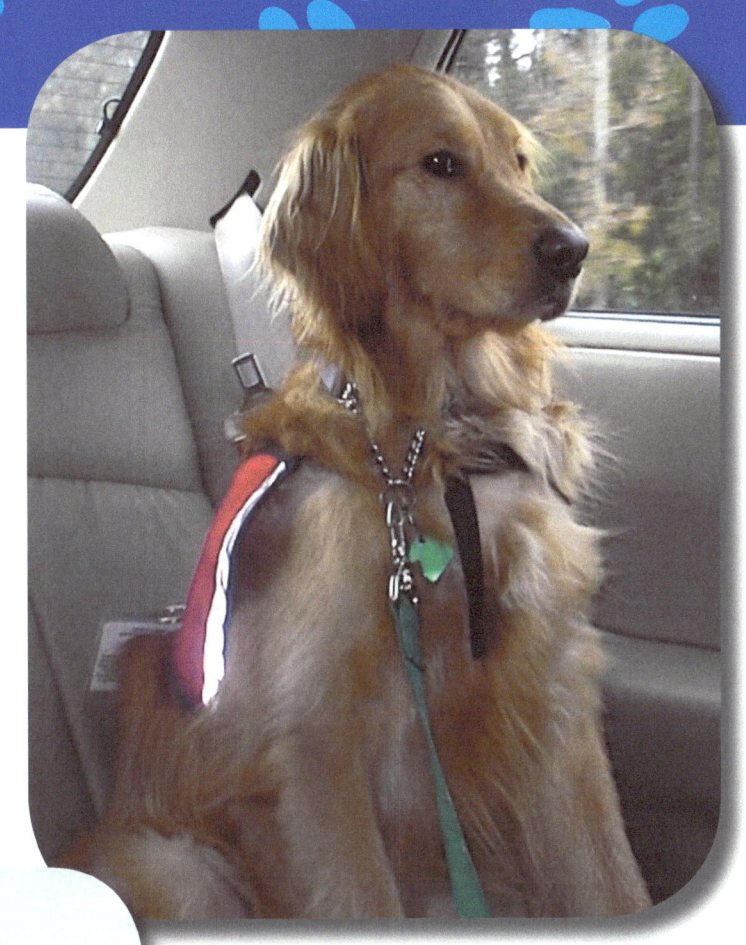

I love riding in automobiles, especially when somebody rolls down the window on my side. I put my head out the window to feel the wind on my face. I also enjoy watching cars drive by and seeing the people in the cars smiling back at me with delight.

Once we got to the movie theatre, Adam used his wheelchair and I happily jogged along very close to him. I was in line next to Adam waiting to buy our movie tickets, when someone began to pet me. I was confused, wondering if I was allowed to play, since someone was petting me. Adam instructed me to ignore the stranger and then asked the stranger to "certainly admire Casper but please do not pet her! She is on duty." That reminded me that I was in a public place and not at home, where I am allowed to play. Even though my working coat says DO NOT PET, sometimes people cannot resist touching me.

Adam decided to buy popcorn from the concession stand before the movie started. The lady behind the counter said "That will be $2.50 please." Adam gave the lady a five dollar bill. She placed two one dollar bills and two quarters in Adam's hand for change. As Adam was attempting to put the change into his pocket, he dropped a quarter on the floor, where it rolled several feet before coming to a

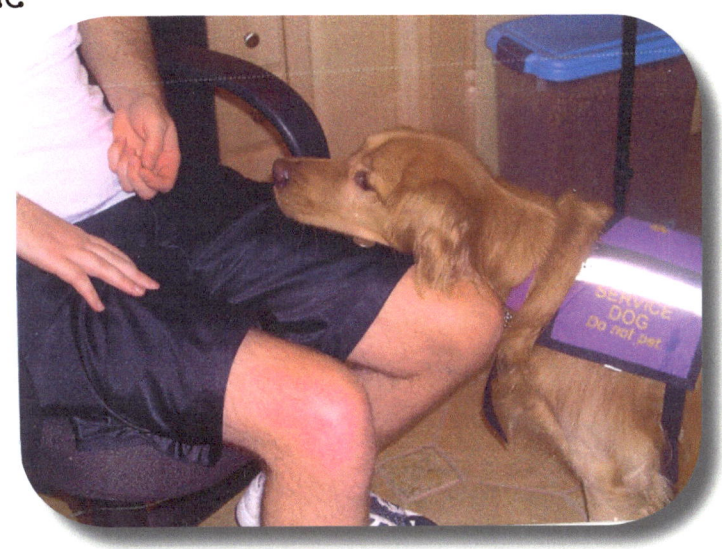

stop. "Casper, look!" Adam said, while pointing at the quarter. "Get it!" I quickly trotted over to the quarter, picked it up with my teeth, and took the coin directly to Adam, where I gently laid it on his lap. Adam lavishly praised me and gave me a few scratches on my head, while the onlookers, who I captivated immediately, began to clap in amazement of my talents.

Once in the theatre, I lay silently against Adam's feet hoping to find some popcorn on the floor to eat. I usually watch the movie for the first ten minutes or so and then I close my eyes and rest. Suddenly a loud bang startled me. I immediately sat straight up, staring at Adam. "It's okay", he assured me, while stroking my head. "That was just the movie, don't worry." I laid back down beside Adam once he assured me everything was okay.

When the movie is over, I am back on duty, walking next to Adam, and passing up any kernels of popcorn that people dropped on the floor. Though I could easily swoop up the popcorn from the floor, Adam reminds me that I am not allowed to eat anything on the ground because it is unsanitary and might upset my tummy. Now, back at our car, I watch Adam until he gives me permission to jump into my seat. I will not jump in until Adam tells me to, just in case he is still holding onto my leash because I could hurt his hand that way. Turning into our driveway, Adam hollers, "We're home!" Adam's father takes the wheelchair out of the trunk while I remain in the car. I always stay in the car until Adam is ready for me to hop out.

I open the front door by pulling a rope attached to the door handle and walk backwards until the latch swings open. It is my job to go into the house first and then turn around and wait for Adam, watching, in case he needs my help.

Once we are both inside, I close the door by pushing it with my nose until it is shut tightly.

After a lengthy drink of water from my bowl, I returned to find Adam lounging on the couch. He grinned at me saying, "Casper look," while pointing in the direction of a table several feet away. "Get the remote," Understanding him completely, I went over to the remote, picked it up in my mouth, carried it to Adam and dropped it gently on his lap.

After thanking me, Adam asked if I would like to lie next to him on the couch. This is one of my favorite rewards! Now I can lie beside him and rest until our next fun-filled day together!

I stay with Adam at all times because I am a working service dog and it is my job to take care of him.

The End

www.ingramcontent.com/pod-product-compliance
Ingram Content Group UK Ltd.
Pitfield, Milton Keynes, MK11 3LW, UK
UKHW060137240426
12048UKWH00002B/80